J 629.133
Olien
Olien, Rebecca

Rescue Helicopters in Action

First Facts®

Transportation Zone

Rescue Helicopters in Action

by Becky Olien

CAPSTONE PRESS
a capstone imprint

First Facts is published by Capstone Press,
151 Good Counsel Drive, P.O. Box 669, Mankato, Minnesota 56002.
www.capstonepub.com

 Books published by Capstone Press are manufactured with paper
containing at least 10 percent post-consumer waste.

Library of Congress Cataloging-in-Publication Data
Olien, Rebecca.
  Rescue helicopters in action/by Becky Olien.
     p. cm.—(First facts. Transportation zone)
  Includes bibliographical references and index.
  Summary: "Discusses the history, function, and workings of rescue helicopters"—
Provided by publisher.
  ISBN 978-1-4296-6850-7 (library binding)
  1. Helicopters in search and rescue operations—Juvenile literature. 2. Emergency
vehicles—Juvenile literature. 3. Helicopters—Juvenile literature. I. Title.
  TL553.8.O45 2012
  629.133′352—dc22   2010054616

Editorial Credits
Karen L. Daas and Anthony Wacholtz, editors; Gene Bentdahl, designer; Eric Gohl,
    media researcher; Laura Manthe, production specialist

Image Credits
Alamy/Frymire Archive, 9
Capstone Studio/Karon Dubke, 22
DVIC/U.S. Coast Guard/PO2 Etta Smith, 21
Getty Images Inc./Gamma-Keystone, 10; Time & Life Pictures/Frank Scherschel, 13
iStockphoto/fabphoto, 15
Shutterstock/Brian Finestone, 1; Bruce C. Murray, cover; David Mee, 5; Graham Taylor,
    16; Kameel4u, 19; William Attard McCarthy, 6

Printed in the United States of America in North Mankato, Minnesota.
032011   006110CGF11

Table of Contents

Rescue Helicopters

Whoosh! Blades whirl as a rescue helicopter zooms through the sky. Rescue helicopters help people who are trapped or hurt. They save people from floods, fires, and other emergencies. Rescue helicopters also carry hurt people to hospitals.

6

Rescue Helicopter Crews

Rescue helicopter crew members work together. The pilot flies the helicopter. The co-pilot helps the pilot **navigate**. A winchman lowers a cable to people on the ground or in the water. A crew member can be lowered on the cable to help the victims. Medics take care of people who are hurt.

navigate: to decide the direction a vehicle should travel

Before the Rescue Helicopter

Rescue helicopters weren't invented until the 1900s. Until then, people used cars, boats, and airplanes to rescue people. But these vehicles often could not reach people in remote places. Many of these people could not be helped.

9

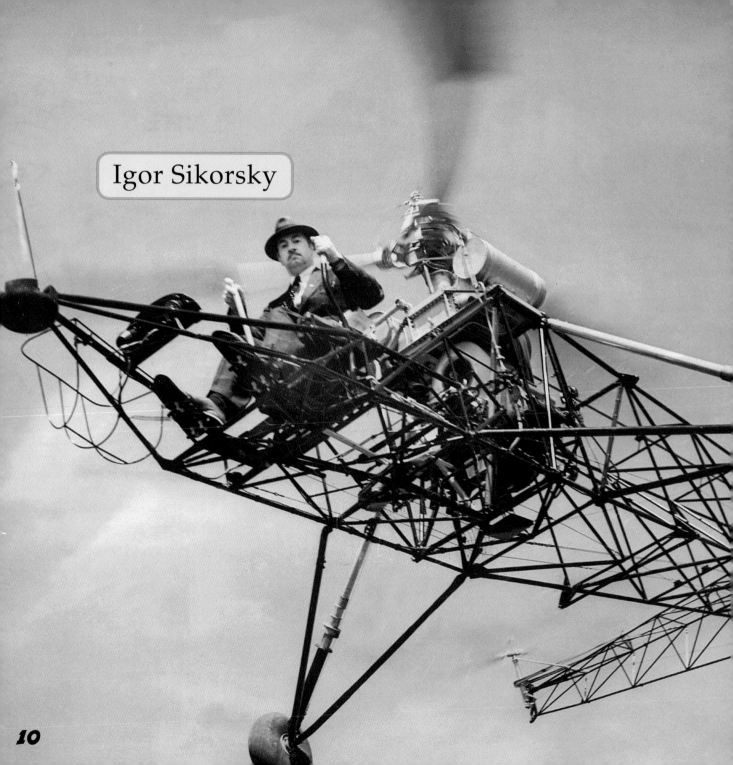

Igor Sikorsky

Inventors of the Helicopter

To reach people in difficult places, a different aircraft was needed. In 1907 Paul Cornu of France invented the first helicopter. It stayed in the air for 20 seconds. In 1939 Igor Sikorsky of Russia built a helicopter that could fly long distances.

Early Rescue Helicopters

Early rescue helicopters did not have much power. They could not carry heavy loads. These helicopters could rescue only one person at a time. But they could rise and drop in a straight line. The helicopters could reach areas that other aircraft could not.

13

Rescue Helicopters Today

Today rescue helicopters are larger and faster. A **GPS** helps the crew travel to the right location. The helicopters drop rescue collars or baskets to pick up people. Rescue helicopters carry people to hospitals faster than ambulances and boats can. These helicopters have medical equipment for people who are hurt.

GPS: an electronic tool used to find the location of an object

rotors

cockpit

landing skid

light

Parts of a Rescue Helicopter

Each part of a rescue helicopter was designed for a purpose. Some rescue helicopters have a main rotor and a tail rotor. Other rescue helicopters have two large main rotors. The pilot controls the helicopter from the **cockpit**. Lights help the crew search for people at night. A rescue helicopter has landing skids or wheels to touch down on ground.

cockpit: the area in a rescue helicopter where the pilot sits

How a Rescue Helicopter Works

Many parts work together to get a rescue helicopter off the ground and moving. An engine turns a rescue helicopter's rotors. Spinning rotors lift the rescue helicopter into the air. The pilot uses control sticks and pedals in the cockpit. They control the helicopter's direction and speed. Rescue helicopters can also **hover** in the air.

hover: to stay in one place in the air

cockpit

Rescue Helicopter Facts

- Rescue helicopters land at hospitals. Workers move hurt people from the rescue helicopter into the hospital.

- The U.S. Coast Guard uses rescue helicopters to help people in the water. They also save people from burning or sinking ships.

- The U.S. military's rescue helicopters help injured soldiers. The crew lands or lowers a rope or basket to the injured soldier. The crew then lifts the soldier into the helicopter.

- Rescue helicopter crews save animals too. They have rescued dogs, bears, and even crocodiles.

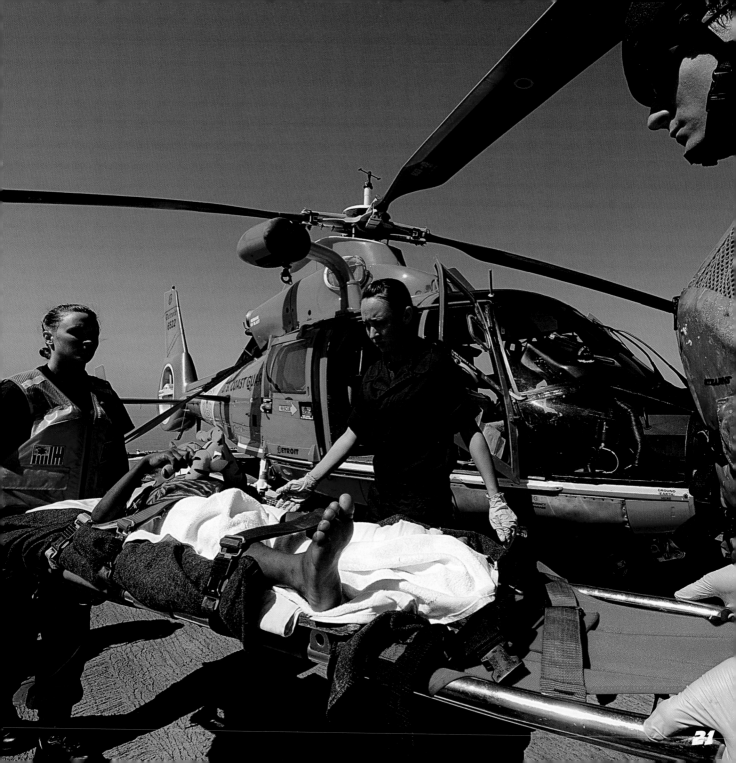

Hands On: Make a Whirly Bird

The first idea for a helicopter came from a flying toy top made in China long ago. Other flying toys helped people invent the helicopter. Some, like this whirly bird, had feathers.

What You Need

3 feathers	toothpick
1-inch (2.5-centimeter)	plastic straw
Styrofoam ball	a windy day
marker	

What You Do

1. Poke the feathers into the Styrofoam ball so they are the same distance apart.
2. Two of the feathers are the bird's wings. The other feather is its tail. Draw a face with a marker between the two wings.
3. Stick the toothpick in the bottom of the ball.
4. Place the toothpick in the end of the plastic straw.
5. Hold the straw up so the whirly bird catches the wind.
6. Watch as the wind lifts the bird from the straw.

The feather wings and tail are like the rotors of a helicopter. As they spin, they lift the whirly bird into the air.

Glossary

cockpit (KOK-pit)—the area in a rescue helicopter where the pilot sits

GPS (JEE PEE ESS)—an electronic tool used to find the location of an object; GPS stands for global positioning system

hover (HUHV-ur)—to stay in one place in the air

medic (MED-ik)—a person who is trained to help injured people; paramedics and emergency medical technicians are medics

navigate (NAV-uh-gate)—to decide the direction a vehicle should travel

pilot (PYE-luht)—a person who flies a helicopter or other aircraft

remote (ri-MOHT)—hard to reach

Read More

Aloian, Molly. *Hovering Helicopters.* Vehicles on the Move. New York: Crabtree, Pub. Company, 2011**.**

Lindeen, Mary. *Helicopters.* Mighty Machines. Minneapolis: Bellwether Media, 2008.

Internet Sites

FactHound offers a safe, fun way to find Internet sites related to this book. All of the sites on FactHound have been researched by our staff.

Here's all you do:

Visit *www.facthound.com*

Type in this code: 9781429668507

Check out projects, games and lots more at
www.capstonekids.com

Index